Your Lungs

by Anne Ylvisaker

Consultant:
Marjorie Hogan, M.D.
Associate Professor of Pediatrics, University of Minnesota
Pediatrician, Hennepin County Medical Center

Bridgestone Books

an imprint of Capstone Press
Mankato, Minnesota

Bridgestone Books are published by Capstone Press
151 Good Counsel Drive, P.O. Box 669, Mankato, Minnesota 56002
http://www.capstone-press.com

Library of Congress Cataloging-in-Publication Data
Ylvisaker, Anne.
    Your lungs/by Anne Ylvisaker.
    p. cm.—(Bridgestone science library)
    Includes bibliographical references and index.
    Summary: Introduces the lungs and their makeup, their function within
the respiratory system, asthma, and how to keep lungs healthy.
    ISBN 0-7368-1149-4
    1. Lungs—Juvenile literature. [1. Lungs.] I. Title. II. Series.
QP121 .Y58 2002
612.2—dc21
                                                                2001003595

Editorial Credits
Rebecca Glaser, editor; Karen Risch, product planning editor; Linda Clavel, cover and
    interior layout designer and illustrator; Alta Schaffer, photo researcher; Nancy White,
    photo stylist

Photo Credits
Capstone Press/Gary Sundermeyer, cover (all), 1, 4, 14, 18, 20
©Eye of Science, SPL, Photo Researchers, Inc., 16

**Bridgestone Books thanks South Central Technical College, North Mankato, Minnesota,
for providing medical models used in photos.**

1 2 3 4 5 6 07 06 05 04 03 02

Table of Contents

Your Lungs

Lungs are the organs you use to breathe. They bring fresh air into your body. Lungs take used air out of your body. You have one lung on each side of your heart.

organ

a part of the body that does a job; the heart and lungs are examples of organs

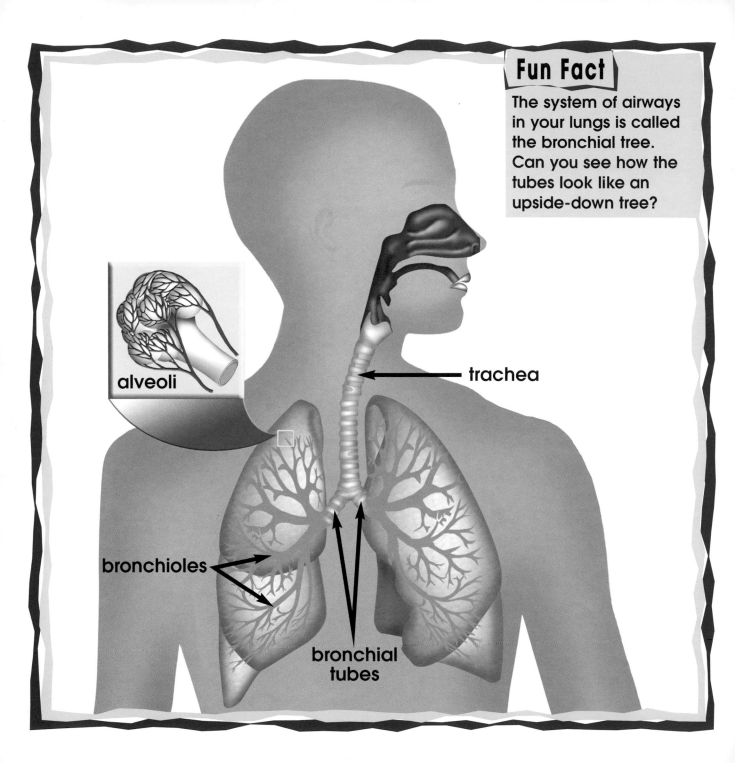

alveoli

trachea

bronchioles

bronchial tubes

Inside Your Lungs

Thousands of airways branch through your lungs. The trachea splits into two bronchial tubes. One tube goes into each lung. The bronchial tubes branch into smaller tubes called bronchioles. The bronchioles end at tiny air sacs called alveoli (al-VEE-uh-lie).

trachea
the airway that connects the nose and mouth to the lungs

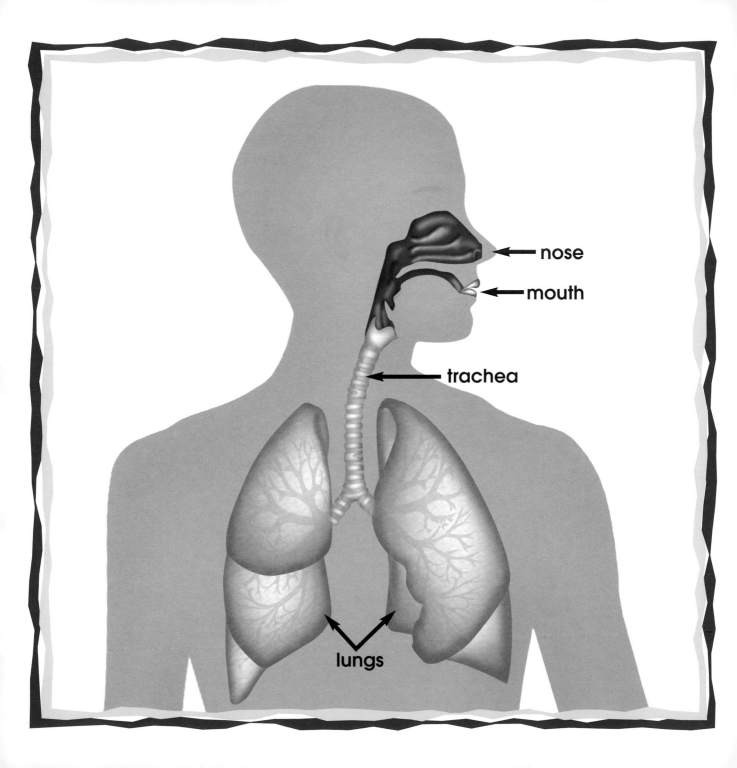

Your Respiratory System

Your body needs oxygen to live. Oxygen is a colorless gas in the air. The respiratory system moves air in and out of your body. Your nose, mouth, trachea, and lungs are the main parts of your respiratory system.

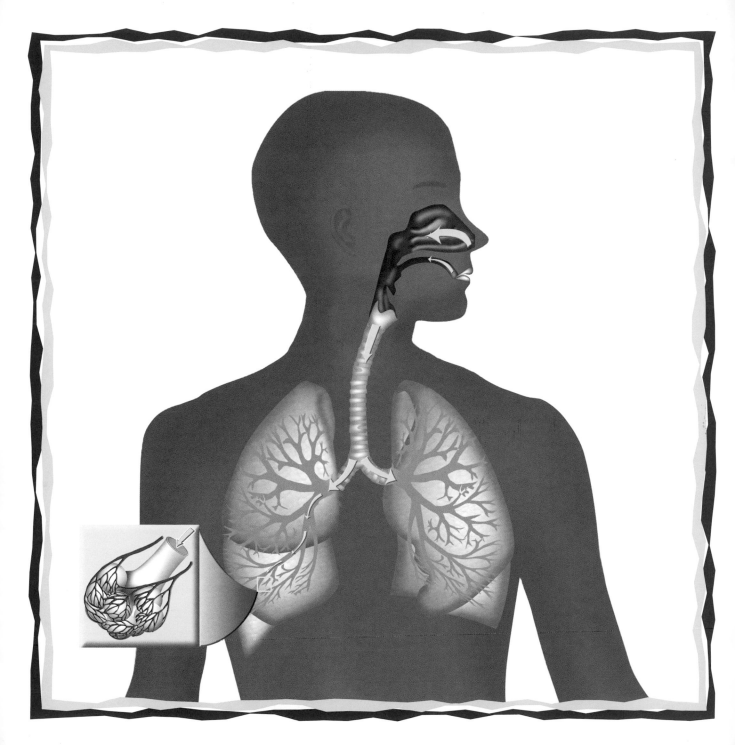

Breathing In

When you breathe in, air enters your nose and mouth. Air then travels through the trachea, bronchial tubes, and bronchioles. The air ends up at the alveoli.

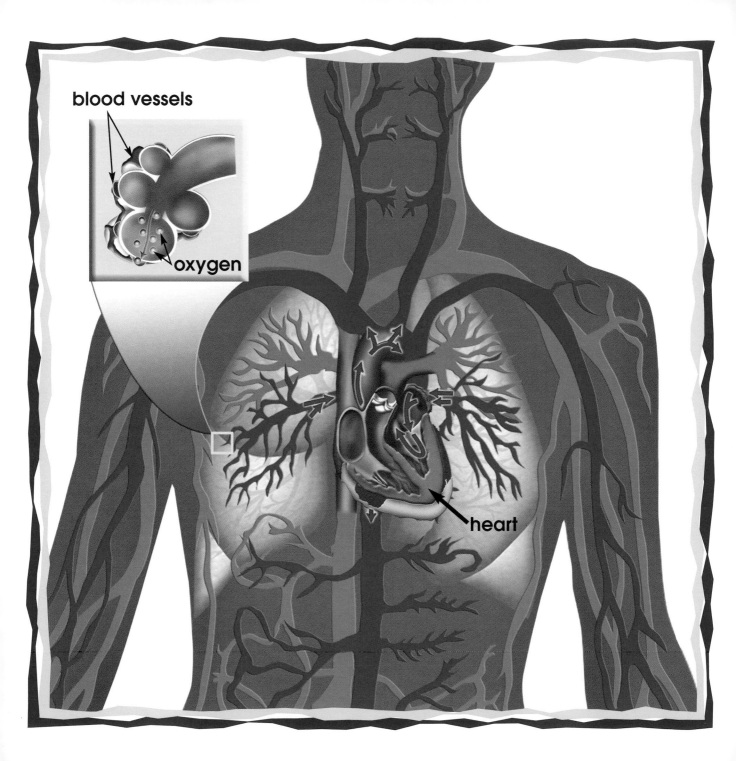

blood vessels

oxygen

heart

Oxygen Goes to Your Body

Oxygen travels through the thin walls of the alveoli into small blood vessels. Blood carries oxygen to your heart through these tiny tubes. The heart then pumps this blood to your whole body.

blood vessel
a tube that carries blood throughout your body

Breathing Out

Your body makes carbon dioxide after it uses oxygen. Your body does not need carbon dioxide. Blood carries carbon dioxide back to your heart and lungs. The carbon dioxide leaves your body when you breathe out.

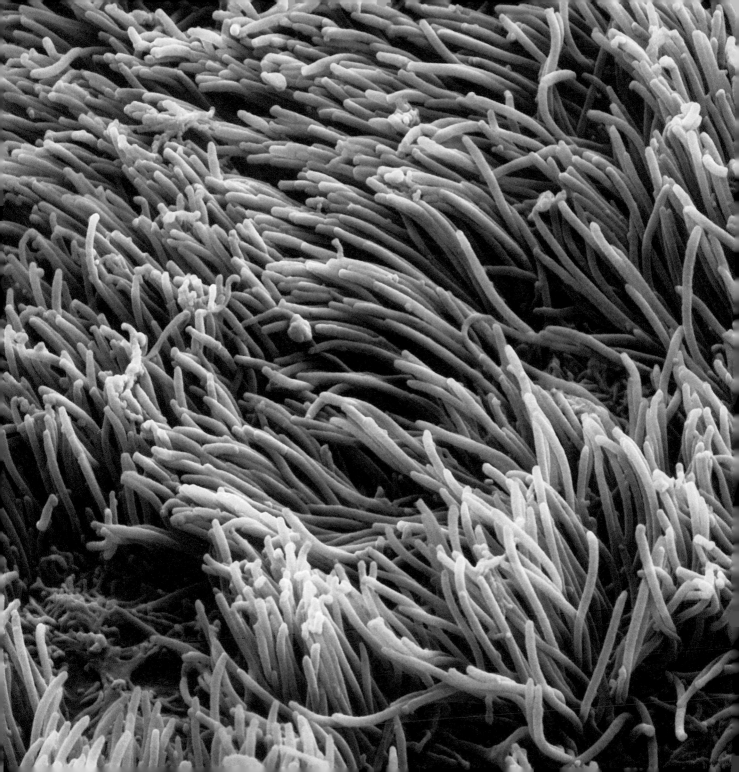

Self-Cleaning Lungs

Your nose and your bronchial tubes have cleaners called cilia. These tiny hairs move back and forth to catch dirt. This dirt goes out of your body when you sneeze or cough. Pollution and cigarette smoke can weaken the cilia. More dirt then gets into your lungs.

pollution
harmful matter that makes the air, water, or land dirty

17

Asthma

Many people have a condition called asthma (AZ-muh). Dust, hot or cold air, or exercising might give them trouble breathing. People with asthma breathe in medicine from an inhaler. The medicine opens their bronchial tubes.

inhaler

a small device from which you breathe in medicine through your mouth

Fun Fact

Babies are born with pink lungs. Breathing pollution makes lungs change color. Adults have gray-white lungs. Smokers may have black lungs.

Healthy Lungs

You can keep your lungs healthy. Exercise makes your respiratory system stronger. Exercise increases the amount of air you can take into your lungs. Staying away from cigarette smoke keeps your lungs clean.

Hands On: Count Your Breaths

How many times do you breathe each minute?

What You Need

Stopwatch or clock with a second hand
Paper and pencil

What You Do

1. Guess how many times you breathe each minute. Write down your guess on the paper.
2. Breathe normally. Put your hand on your chest and count how many times your chest rises in one minute.
3. Write down the number of times. Was it close to your guess?
4. Now exercise for a few minutes. Run up and down the stairs, ride your bike, or take a fast walk.
5. Count your breaths for another minute. How many breaths do you take in one minute now? Write down that number.

You breathe harder when you exercise. Your lungs take in more oxygen. Your muscles need the extra oxygen when they work hard.

Words to Know

alveoli (al-VEE-uh-lie)—tiny air sacs at the ends of bronchioles in the lungs

bronchial tubes (BRAHNG-kee-uhl TOOBZ)—the two airways that split off from the trachea and enter each lung

carbon dioxide (KAHR-buhn dye-AHK-side)—a colorless gas that people and animals breathe out

cilia (SIL-ee-uh)—short hairs that line the airways of the lungs

oxygen (OK-suh-juhn)—a colorless gas in air that humans and animals need to live

trachea (TRAY-kee-uh)—the air passage that connects the nose and the mouth to the lungs

Read More

Lee, Justin. *The Respiratory System.* Insider's Guide to the Body. New York: Rosen, 2001.

Maurer, Tracy. *Heart and Lungs.* Bodyworks. Vero Beach, Fla.: Rourke, 1999.

Stille, Darlene R. *The Respiratory System.* A True Book. New York: Children's Press, 1997.

Internet Sites

BrainPOP
http://www.brainpop.com/health/respiratory/respiration/
  index.weml
The Lung Association Student Index
http://www.sk.lung.ca/education/student/student.html
Your Gross and Cool Body—Respiratory System
http://yucky.kids.discovery.com/flash/body/pg000138.html

Index